YOUR KNOWLEDGE HAS VALUE

Bibliographic information published by the German National Library:

The German National Library lists this publication in the National Bibliography; detailed bibliographic data are available on the Internet at http://dnb.dnb.de .

Imprint:

Copyright © 2016 GRIN Verlag, Open Publishing GmbH
Print and binding: Books on Demand GmbH, Norderstedt Germany
ISBN: 9783668352131

This book at GRIN:

http://www.grin.com/en/e-book/344845/potential-risk-and-loss-of-online-banking-with-smartphone-applications

Selina Kolls

Potential Risk and Loss of Online Banking with Smartphone Applications. A FAIR Analysis

GRIN Publishing

FAIR Analysis

Frequency and Magnitude of Future Loss associated with Online Banking Application

through Smartphones

Contents

Fair Analysis

In today's dynamic and competitive environment, new and improved technology and innovations tend to shape our business and social environment. As the fast and emerging technological advancements continue to grow, it remains to pose a significant amount of risks when deployed to businesses and organizations. Impaired IT controls can have significant effects on the organizations' performance and profitability. Companies are now tasked to employ the latest and modest technologies, or they risk losing business and market share. Similarly, consumers are not left to chance with the innovations. With the ease of access to the internet and mobile phones, individuals can now use these platforms and tools for making utility payments, banking, shopping and even budgeting. Given the increasing pace of expansion in the mobile finance sector, it will be possible for individuals to conduct online banking applications through their smartphones. However, the rapid developments of these tools, devices, and their functionality concerning introducing m-commerce supporting technologies, will create newer risks, including cyber criminal activities which are increasing by the day and made worse by the economic challenges.

To help control and manage these IT exposures, Freund & Jones (2015) developed a FAIR approach to aid businesses to measure and control information risks. The FAIR analysis, which stands for Factor Analysis of Information Risk, is an international standard quantitative method for handling operational risks and cyber security. This technique is mostly used to identify, understand, assess and measure information risk in meaningful financial context (Freund & Jones, 2015). It creates a basis for establishing an accurate model to information risk management. The power of FAIR is relatively massive as it helps risk professionals to foster clarity and generate viable decisions from the ambiguous risky environment one was exposed to and basing judgment on useful measurements that yield quantifiable and defensible outcomes. The objective of this paper is to analyze the frequencies and magnitude of present and future losses associated with online banking systems applications.

Loss scenario, threat agent, and risk question identified

We are shifting from the paper-based banking environment that has been in existence for a very long time to a digital trading platform that is still in its early stages but seeks to provide real-time processing and convenience. Internet development has become the common source of communication across the globe and is rapidly being used by all banks as a network for offering products and services to customers and receiving instructions (CMFS, 2016). Different financial institutions employ various mechanisms for providing services over the internet. Today, most people do not need to use a computer to facilitate transactions and manage accounts, instead, widespread of mobile phones with banking applications has made it possible for people to transfer funds, make payments and keep track of finances (Lyne, 2014). But the questions that mirror in our minds are, are these banking apps safe? Is it the safest way to manage accounts? Numerous threat agents consist of the malicious software, malware attacks through the internet and intranet, hacking, phishing, viruses and worms that may infect systems and mobile phones. These attacks and infections are deemed to be more enhanced and may be of higher threats in the coming years.

Below, is a chart illustrating the usage of mobile phone transactions by brand.

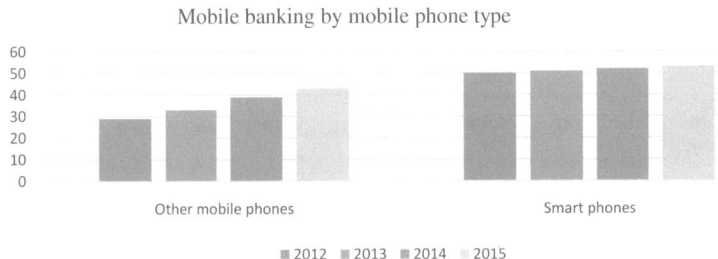

Figure 1: Source: Consumers and Mobile Financial Services 2016, Board of Governors of the Federal Reserve System, March 2016, download from
https://www.federalreserve.gov/communitydev/mobile_finance.htm, p. 6, Fig. 1.

Most financial institutions allow their smartphones users' customers to log into their internet banking websites while others offer banking application systems that enable customers to keep track of their money using their mobile phones. With new and rapid improvements on Android Trojan infections, worms and virus problems may exist in mobile phones with multiple applications such as the iPhone 5 which may pose a high threat when users use them to access their bank accounts. This is so, since, with several running programs there are greater risks that malicious software may be running without the user's knowledge (Martin, 2016). But do the users have antivirus for their phone and do they need one if they don't? Additional programs in mobile phones may attack protected information as well as the communication channels with internal control systems mechanisms. Also, text updates services send notifications of an accounts balance or mini statements in the form of text messages. There is a likelihood of enormous risks as they do not provide direct access to one's account (Lyne, 2014). This prompts the question, are these updates safe?

Another challenge is associated with hackers and scammers. There have been cases where customers check their account balances online and can claim that there are funds, however, when they make a transaction, their debit cards are declined due to insufficient funds. Are such cases, incidences of scammers? We might say it's an online trap. To some, it may never be easy to check account balances, but we try this every time on our mobile phones, and the text message display portrays false sense on customers. On the other hand, businesses too are at high risks of losing vital and confidential data, ERP integration challenges, identity and security problems and application development issues. Threats to internal control systems emanate from attacks which can cause immense damages to ICS (Lyne, 2014).

Current state FAIR analysis to estimate current loss

Information technology developments are rarely protected, and privacy is not entirely guaranteed. Given numerous surveys, research, data breached reports, the cost of information breached, facts and statistics, there exists too much of information and inadequacy of significant and useful data. For this reason, FAIR approach was developed to quantify and manage information risk of any scope and intricacy (Freund & Jones, 2015). For banking institutions, the FAIR analysis will serve as a risk management improvement tool. Key security firms that identify and investigate incidences and reports by various clients have issued estimates of loss suffered by individuals and businesses annually. If the effects of the threats to online banking and related platforms are extended to public and government enterprises as well as the population, it is relatively easy to estimate that the number of damages increases to billions of funds (Martin, 2016).

Most of the online banking threats and cybercrime activities are assumed to originate in some form of planned activities. The act is becoming more of a business opportunity for individuals driven by personal gains (CMFS, 2016). A recent primary concern is where an unknown source has been luring customers to accidentally show their bank account details. In such cases, emails were sent to clients stating that their account details required renewing and thus, they were to follow certain procedures their accounts would be renewed (Lyne, 2014). Given that most customers were unaware that such scams could ever happen, they were able to reveal their login details, passwords and account information to the criminals. FAIR approach seeks to teach consumers on how to use modern internet security solutions that may protect their devices against malicious software and related threats. Likewise, bank clients are required to update mobile phones programs and applications regularly, use complex passwords, protect personal information, and be aware of the scareware attacks.

Apparently, numerous security options are being looked at systematically and enhanced. The FAIR analysis stands to provide the best practices intended to strengthen the security mechanisms within mobile phones and banks ICS component. For businesses, the information security management system for the internal control systems operations must be understood as a crucial element of a superior management system of a bank. The system will also take into consideration the risks and offer strategies to prevent, conduct checks, maintain and to improve the ICS. As part of the FAIR analysis, the approach will aid banks to set up security functions. This serves to define the roles and responsibilities for the safety of the ICS components. Similarly, they should facilitate establishment and maintenance of documentations. Information and records regarding the security of the ICS functions should be developed, maintained and protected from unauthorized access. Another vital aspect is the risk management; here, every function and resource of an internal control system should be carefully considered, properly examined and assessed. As threats continue to change and grow, continuous countermeasures are needed to keep off possible attacks.

Policy improvement proposal

There is an increased need for banks to safeguard the security of their customers. This can be effected through passwords, server, and firewall security as well as encryption (Infosec Institute, 2013). Use of passwords and usernames are one of the important aspects for improving online security as they assure that those authorized have access to their own accounts (Martin, 2016). Needless to say, scammers and hackers have sophisticated ways to capture PINs and usernames during transmission and use them to access their victim's accounts. As such, there is a need to facilitate secure and efficient authentication models since trust issues, and security breaches have gained new dimensions in financial services. Numerous new models including policy identification, server analysis and network analysis techniques to detect and control fraudulent activities should be developed, and the existing models should be improved for use in the online banking landscapes.

Post policy implementation of FAIR analysis

The FAIR approach seeks to provide avenues for individuals and banks to quantify and manage risks. At the same time, it gives proper guidelines for implementing policies deployed. Where security policies prevail, the designers must assess to see whether this will influence the design of the solution. The developer needs to evaluate if the policy developed can identify those assets that need adequate protection and also identify the possible scammers and hackers; this provides an insight into the magnitude of trust given to the internal and external users (Infosec Institute, 2013). The results of the implementation process will aid to evaluate the policies' accuracy and broadness. Also, the designers are capable of recognizing potential policy improvements that can be amended and modified.

Costs and benefits of the policy

To balance the costs and benefits of the various countermeasures is in itself an act of risk analysis. This helps to identify and evaluate those assets, threats to the properties, the potential loss that the entities and individuals have been exposed to and how the losses have been managed. Banks must be able to assess the values to their assets. These values are usually based on the cost of replacing the asset when addressing a hardware problem, or the recovery costs when dealing with a software issue. The assessor must also consider how these assets are being utilized, for instance, there may be damages to two computers where one is used by a salesperson to store less valuable information while the other is employed by an accountant to store valuable and confidential data. Banks should also take into consideration the outcomes of breach of security on customer goodwill as well as the brand's image. The costs that materialize should help in providing an idea of the amounts spent to fend off these threats. Evaluating risks and developing appropriate countermeasures is crucial to the lifecycle of assets protection. In the end, it is of significant benefits to the organization and the customers as they will derive improved brand image, increased customer goodwill, and trust.

Normative analysis and position argued

Much of what is being conducted in our daily lives is being trailed and documented in the online platforms. While there may exist an information and activities that are not distributed online, in future, this is likely to diminish. The new and improved Android tools and applications comprise a huge number of entry points. As such, there are increased opportunities to compromise these devices through sophisticated ways (Martin, 2016). In recent times, mobile phones risks and threats are mostly targeted at individuals rather than organizations. These attacks are predicted to take advantage of the mobile phone platforms today and in the years to come. Smartphone users are less aware of the possible dangers and threats they are exposed to. As such, they are strongly recommended to use antivirus programs on their devices (Lyne, 2014) as the banks and other organization are establishing ways to develop and implement policies to curb online risks, promote and support online security education and raising awareness for users which will be of significant benefits to the customers.

Rationale behind each FAIR element

Most of these risk and threats are facilitated by internet hacking, improper use of company assets and network and device vulnerabilities. An understanding and awareness of the various weaknesses and exposures is crucial for the success of network functions. Identification policies and procedures will aid eliminate potential risks. This helps by recognizing and certifying authorized users from attackers. Person and entities are identified by using categories e.g. customers of a particular organization, employees, and business partners. This ensures that the policymakers have formulated all possible risks and threats and have not passed over on vital threats. To develop high levels of security assurance, banks must deploy viable and robust mechanisms to eliminate points of failure (Infosec Institute, 2013). For this reason, security professionals and designers of policies must work with banks to examine how much investment in resources and security measure is acceptable for assets that need to be safeguarded. Implementing these controls is essential as it will influence mutual support and produce favorable results.

Organizations may establish best practices and tools and training necessary to safeguard network functions. They may employ software devices from Cisco e.g. AutoSecure, other third party platforms e.g. router audit tool and various website resources. These tools steer fast implementation of security policies and processes to facilitate secure networking function. Similarly, banks can identify the role of each server to enable generate informed decisions on the steps that will be enforced to secure host systems. A network may have multiple users and workstations that will require being critically assessed from the inside and external to the network. Those applications and services that are still running on servers must be identified and network functions and ports that are unnecessary need to be blocked. Antivirus software programs must be installed and regularly updated, and hosts should be continuously observed for any signs of mischievous and criminal activities.

Conclusion

Technological advancement comes with both advantages and shortcomings. In the quest to enhance ease of transactions in the banking sector through the use of mobile phones, it is essential to recognize the risks associated with it. It is evident that online banking is growing at a fast rate and this poses security threats to the global economy. Strategies must be formulated to guarantee the safety of online banking. As mentioned earlier, regulations should be put in place to ensure that threats are identified earlier and be addressed. The use of secure phone applications is essential for safe online transactions. Malware that affects the functionality of phones and Trojan programs intended to steal confidential information of users are some of the biggest threats in online banking. The use of malware protection smartphone programs should be encouraged to prevent any form of cyber attack.

References

Consumers and Mobile Financial Services (CMFS) 2016, Board of Governors of the Federal Reserve System, March 2016, download from https://www.federalreserve.gov/communitydev/mobile_finance.htm, p. 6, Fig. 1.

Freund, J., & Jones, J. (2015). *Measuring and managing information risk: A FAIR approach.* Oxford, UK: Butterworth-Heinemann.

Infosec Institute. (2013). 2013 – The Impact of Cybercrime. Retrieved from http://resources.infosecinstitute.com/2013-impact-cybercrime/

Lyne, J. (2014). BBC Consumer. Are mobile banking apps safe? Retrieved from http://www.bbc.co.uk/consumer/25953741

Martin. (2016). Money. Current account guides. Is banking on your smart phone safe? Retrieved from http://www.money.co.uk/current-accounts/is-banking-on-your-smart-phone-safe.htm

YOUR KNOWLEDGE HAS VALUE

- We will publish your bachelor's and master's thesis, essays and papers

- Your own eBook and book - sold worldwide in all relevant shops

- Earn money with each sale

Upload your text at www.GRIN.com
and publish for free